TEAM SPIRIT ®

SMART BOOKS FOR YOUNG FANS

THE SAN FRANCISCO GIANTS

BY
MARK STEWART

NORWOOD HOUSE PRESS
CHICAGO, ILLINOIS

Norwood House Press
P.O. Box 316598
Chicago, Illinois 60631

For information regarding Norwood House Press, please visit our website at:
www.norwoodhousepress.com or call 866-565-2900.

All photos courtesy of Getty Images except the following:
SportsChrome (4, 9, 10, 11, 14, 19), F.W. Rueckheim & Brother (6), Street & Smith Publications, Inc. (7),
Golden Press (15), Author's Collection (16, 21, 26, 34 bottom left), Topps, Inc. (17, 22, 35 top, 36, 40, 43 bottom),
Black Book Partners Archives (23, 25, 29, 34 top, 35 bottom left, 38, 39, 45), Tom DiPace (28),
TIME Inc./Sports Illustrated (31), San Francisco Giants (33), Sweet Caporal (34 bottom right), York Music Co. (37),
SSPC (42 top), Baseball Cards Magazine (42 bottom), Baseball Magazine (43 top), Matt Richman (48).
Cover Photo: Icon Sports Media

The memorabilia and artifacts pictured in this book are presented for educational and informational purposes,
and come from the collection of the author.

Editor: Mike Kennedy
Designer: Ron Jaffe
Project Management: Black Book Partners, LLC.
Special thanks to Topps, Inc.

Library of Congress Cataloging-in-Publication Data

Stewart, Mark, 1960-
  The San Francisco Giants / by Mark Stewart. -- Library ed.
      p. cm. -- (Team spirit)
  Includes bibliographical references and index.
  Summary: "A Team Spirit Baseball edition featuring the San Francisco
Giants that chronicles the history and accomplishments of the team. Includes
access to the Team Spirit website, which provides additional information,
updates and photos"--Provided by publisher.
  ISBN 978-1-59953-496-1 (library : alk. paper) -- ISBN 978-1-60357-376-4
(ebook) 1. San Francisco Giants (Baseball team)--History--Juvenile
literature. I. Title.
  GV875.S34S84 2012
  796.357'640979461--dc23
                                           2011047977

Manufactured in the United States of America in North Mankato, Minnesota.
196N—012012

COVER PHOTO: The Giants celebrate a victory on their home field.

TABLE OF CONTENTS

CHAPTER	PAGE
MEET THE GIANTS	4
GLORY DAYS	6
HOME TURF	12
DRESSED FOR SUCCESS	14
WE WON!	16
GO-TO GUYS	20
CALLING THE SHOTS	24
ONE GREAT DAY	26
LEGEND HAS IT	28
IT REALLY HAPPENED	30
TEAM SPIRIT	32
TIMELINE	34
FUN FACTS	36
TALKING BASEBALL	38
GREAT DEBATES	40
FOR THE RECORD	42
PINPOINTS	44
GLOSSARY	46
EXTRA INNINGS	47
INDEX	48

ABOUT OUR GLOSSARY

In this book, there may be several words that you are reading for the first time. Some are sports words, some are new vocabulary words, and some are familiar words that are used in an unusual way. All of these words are defined on page 46. Throughout the book, sports words appear in **bold type**. Regular vocabulary words appear in ***bold italic type***.

MEET THE GIANTS

When baseball is called the "national pastime," it means that people like watching and playing the game from coast to coast. No team is a better example of this than the San Francisco Giants. They play on the West Coast today, but they began on the East Coast more than 100 years ago.

The players who wear the black and orange of the Giants are part of a tradition that dates back to the 1880s. They play hard and have fun. Many of today's Giants would feel right at home sharing the field with the players from the old days.

This book tells the story of the Giants. They have played a part in many unforgettable moments. They are an important part of American sports. Every season, the Giants take the field hoping to add another chapter to their amazing story.

The Giants rush the mound after their 2010 championship. The first time the team stood atop the baseball world was more than 100 years ago, in 1888.

GLORY DAYS

The Giants played their first game in San Francisco in 1958. Back then, they were baseball's newest "old" team. Their roots stretched back 75 years and thousands of miles to New York City, where they began as the Gothams in 1883. Their proud manager, Jim Mutrie, called his players "giants." Soon that became the name of the team.

Cracker Jack BALL PLAYERS

MCGRAW, NEW YORK - NATIONALS

The Giants were the best team in baseball during the late 1880s. Tim Keefe and Mickey Welch led the pitching staff. Buck Ewing, John Ward, and Roger Connor were the stars on offense. The team won two **pennants** in the **National League (NL)** and helped baseball become the country's most popular sport.

The Giants rose to the top of the NL again in the early part of the 20th century. From 1904 to 1924, they finished first or second 16 times. Their manager during those glory years was John McGraw, who was known as the smartest man

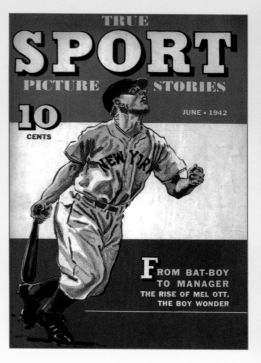

in baseball when he played. As a manager, McGraw was even smarter.

McGraw also had a roster of great players. Christy Mathewson, Joe McGinnity, George Wiltse, Red Ames, Rube Marquard, and Jesse Barnes were among the finest pitchers in the league. The Giants' best hitters included Roger Bresnahan, Larry Doyle, Ross Youngs, George Kelly, Dave Bancroft, and Frankie Frisch. McGraw's teams captured 10 pennants and won the **World Series** three times.

During the 1930s, the Giants won three more pennants. They were led by hitting stars Mel Ott, Bill Terry, and Travis Jackson. Pitchers Carl Hubbell and Hal Schumacher took care of business on the mound. After struggling during the 1940s, the Giants rebuilt their club in the 1950s. They signed several stars from the **Negro Leagues**, including Monte Irvin, Hank Thompson, and Willie Mays. Many experts consider Mays to be the greatest all-around player of his time.

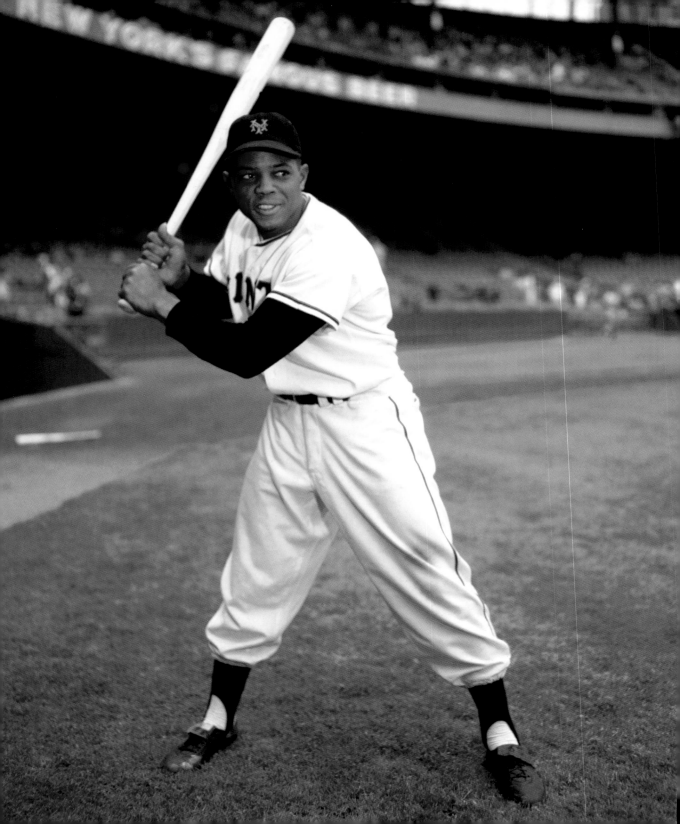

In 1958, the Giants and Brooklyn Dodgers moved to California. The fierce rivalry they started in New York continued on the West Coast. With young power hitters such as Orlando Cepeda, Willie McCovey, and Felipe Alou supporting Mays—and great pitching from Juan Marichal and Gaylord Perry—the Giants continued their winning ways in the 1960s.

San Francisco rose to the top of the standings again in the late 1980s. The Giants were pennant ***contenders*** almost every season. Their heavy hitters included Will Clark, Robby Thompson, Matt Williams, and Kevin Mitchell—and later Barry Bonds and Jeff Kent.

LEFT: Willie Mays strikes a pose in the uniform of the New York Giants.
ABOVE: Barry Bonds watches a home run leave the ballpark.

Mitchell, Bonds, and Kent were each named **Most Valuable Player (MVP)** during this period.

San Francisco also had a great **bullpen**. Rod Beck and Robb Nen were among the best in baseball at closing out games. But the Giants lacked an ace in their **starting rotation**. They could not find a pitcher who could win consistently, like the stars of the past. Still, San Francisco found ways to win. In 2002, the Giants claimed another pennant.

In the years that followed, the Giants relied on *veterans* to help them get back to the World Series. Unfortunately, age and injuries usually ruined their plans. Still, San Francisco fans had a lot to cheer about. In 2007, Bonds hit the 756th home run of his career to become baseball's all-time leader. In 2008 and again in 2009, Tim Lincecum led the NL in strikeouts and won the **Cy Young Award**.

ABOVE: Tim Lincecum   **RIGHT**: Brian Wilson

Lincecum was part of an exciting group of young pitchers that included Matt Cain, Jonathan Sanchez, Madison Bumgarner, and Brian Wilson. They formed the core of a new team that won the World Series in 2010. Other players on that club were Aubrey Huff, Buster Posey, Freddy Sanchez, and Pablo Sandoval. This time the winning formula was good pitching, solid defense, and just enough hitting to get the job done. The Giants had won all of their previous pennants with great lineups full of big-name superstars such as Mathewson and Mays. But in many ways, the 2010 lineup was the greatest of all.

HOME TURF

The Giants have played in three of baseball's most famous stadiums. In New York, their home was the oddly shaped Polo Grounds. A ball hit down the foul lines could travel less than 300 feet and still clear the fence for a home run. A ball hit 400 feet to center field was an easy out.

After moving to San Francisco, the Giants played for 40 years in Candlestick Park. It was built right near the water. "The Stick" was famous for its wind and fog, especially at night.

The Giants opened a new stadium in 2000. Inside and outside, it reminds fans of baseball's best old-time ballparks. Their favorite feature is McCovey Cove, an area in San Francisco Bay just beyond the right field wall. Home runs hit into the water are known as "Splashdowns." No one launched more balls into McCovey Cove than Barry Bonds.

BY THE NUMBERS

- The Giants' stadium has 41,915 seats.
- The distance from home plate to the left field foul pole is 339 feet.
- The distance from home plate to the center field fence is 399 feet.
- The distance from home plate to the right field foul pole is 309 feet.

Paddlers wait for home run balls behind the stadium's right field wall.

For most of their early history, the Giants' colors were red, white, and blue. In some years, the players wore dark blue road uniforms. In 1916, the Giants used a plaid uniform with violet stripes.

CARL HUBBELL
pitcher

Today, the club features orange and black as its colors. They were first used in 1949, when the Giants still played in New York. Back then, the team often had a fancy *NY* on its caps and shirt sleeves.

When the Giants moved across the country, they switched their *NY* to *SF*, which stands for San Francisco. During the 1970s and 1980s, the Giants tried uniform tops that were all black or all orange. In recent years, the players have worn uniforms that look very much like the ones from the 1950s and 1960s.

LEFT: Matt Cain delivers a pitch in the team's road uniform.
ABOVE: Carl Hubbell warms up in the Giants' uniform of the 1930s.

WE WON!

When the Giants beat the Texas Rangers in the 2010 World Series, it marked the eighth time they were champions. The first two seasons the Giants won the World Series—in 1888 and 1889—it was not an official championship. Many record books listed them as six-time champions.

The Giants defeated the St. Louis Browns in 1888 and the Brooklyn Bridegrooms in 1889. The team's top hitters were Buck Ewing, Roger Connor, John Ward, George Gore, and Mike Tiernan. Their leading pitchers were Mickey Welch and Tim Keefe.

The Giants won their first official World Series in 1905. Under the guidance of manager John McGraw, they defeated the Philadelphia Athletics in five games. Each game was a **shutout**. Christy Mathewson had three by himself!

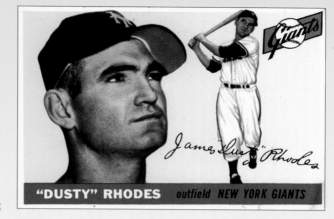

"DUSTY" RHODES *outfield* **NEW YORK GIANTS**

The Giants were champions again in 1921 and 1922. Both times they beat the New York Yankees.

In 1932, McGraw retired. His replacement, Bill Terry, guided the Giants to another championship in 1933. Terry was a **player-manager**. He and Mel Ott were the club's best hitters. Carl Hubbell and Hal Schumacher led the pitching staff. New York beat the Washington Senators in the World Series four games to one.

The Giants' last championship in New York came in 1954. Willie Mays and Dusty Rhodes helped the team defeat the Cleveland Indians in a four-game "sweep." Mays saved the opening game with an amazing catch in center field that fans still talk about. Rhodes had three game-winning hits.

After moving to San Francisco, the Giants won the NL pennant in 1962 and again in 2002. Both times, they lost the World Series in seven exciting games. Finally, after a 56-year wait, Giants fans got to raise the championship flag again in 2010. San Francisco had great pitching all year, but the experts said the team did not have enough hitting to survive in the **postseason**.

In the opening game of the **playoffs** against the Atlanta Braves, the Giants relied on Tim Lincecum. He struck out 14 batters in a 1-0 victory. The only run came on hits by Buster Posey and Cody Ross. Neither had been on the team when the season started. The Giants won two more close games to take the best-of-five series.

In the **National League Championship Series (NLCS)**, Lincecum was brilliant. He won the opening game again, this time with the help of two home runs from Ross.

Matt Cain and Brian Wilson also pitched well in the series, and the Giants defeated the Philadelphia Phillies in six games to win the pennant.

By the time the Giants met the Rangers in the World Series, they felt unbeatable. San Francisco's hitters showed why in the first two games. The Giants scored a total of 20 runs and won each game easily. Texas won Game 3, but the Giants got another amazing performance from a young pitcher in Game 4. A 21-year-old **rookie** named Madison Bumgarner pitched a 4–0 shutout.

The Giants won the series the following day on a three-run homer from 35-year-old Edgar Renteria, another unexpected hero. Renteria had been in the World Series spotlight once before. He had the winning hit for the Florida Marlins in Game 7 of the 1997 World Series. This time, Renteria starred for the Giants and was named the series MVP.

LEFT: Cody Ross flashes a big smile after a home run in Game 1 of the 2010 NLCS.   **ABOVE**: The Giants greet Edgar Renteria after his homer in Game 5 of the 2010 World Series.

To be a true star in baseball, you need more than a quick bat and a strong arm. You have to be a "go-to guy"—someone the manager wants on the pitcher's mound or in the batter's box when it matters most. Fans of the Giants have had a lot to cheer about over the years, including these great stars …

THE PIONEERS

TIM KEEFE   Pitcher

• BORN: 1/1/1857   • DIED: 4/23/1933   • PLAYED FOR TEAM: 1885 TO 1889 & 1891

At a time when many baseball players were often rude and violent, Tim Keefe was called "Sir Timothy" because he was so polite. Keefe won 30 or more games six years in a row for the Giants. After retiring, he coached college baseball at Harvard and Princeton.

CHRISTY MATHEWSON   Pitcher

• BORN: 8/12/1880   • DIED: 10/7/1925   • PLAYED FOR TEAM: 1900 TO 1916

Christy Mathewson was the first true baseball "idol." After graduating from college, he pitched 17 remarkable seasons for the Giants and won 372 games. Mathewson's best pitch was a tailing fastball that he called the "fade-away."

BILL TERRY — First Baseman

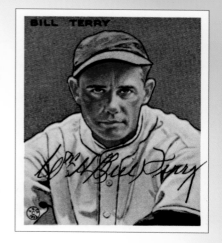

- BORN: 10/30/1898 • DIED: 1/9/1989
- PLAYED FOR TEAM: 1923 TO 1936

Bill Terry saw baseball as a job. He was all business on the field and off it. In 1930, Terry hit .401. In 1932, he became the Giants' player-manager and led the team to the pennant.

MEL OTT — Outfielder

- BORN: 3/2/1909 • DIED: 11/21/1958 • PLAYED FOR TEAM: 1926 TO 1947

Mel Ott went right from high school to the Giants and became the team's most beloved star for two *decades*. At the age of 20, he hit 42 home runs and knocked in 151 runs. Ott retired with 511 homers.

CARL HUBBELL — Pitcher

- BORN: 6/22/1903 • DIED: 11/21/1988 • PLAYED FOR TEAM: 1928 TO 1943

Carl Hubbell threw baseball's best screwball—a pitch that fooled batters by moving in the opposite direction of a curveball. He won more than 20 games each year from 1933 to 1937 and was named NL MVP twice.

WILLIE MAYS — Outfielder

- BORN: 5/6/1931 • PLAYED FOR TEAM: 1951 TO 1972

Willie Mays played baseball in a faster gear than everyone else, yet he almost never made a mistake. He was the NL's strongest hitter, best baserunner, and most spectacular outfielder from the early 1950s to the mid-1960s. Mays ended his career with 660 home runs.

ABOVE: Bill Terry

WILLIE McCOVEY　　　　　First Baseman/Outfielder

• BORN: 1/10/1938　• PLAYED FOR TEAM: 1959 TO 1973 & 1977 TO 1980

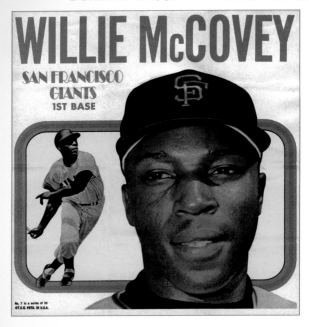

No one in baseball hit the ball harder than Willie McCovey. When he swung and made contact, it sounded like a gunshot. McCovey was loved by Giants fans. He played for the team in four different decades—starting in 1959 and retiring in 1980.

JUAN MARICHAL　　　　Pitcher

• BORN: 10/20/1937

• PLAYED FOR TEAM: 1960 TO 1973

Every pitch Juan Marichal threw was a work of art. He kicked his leg high in the air and then released the ball from any one of a dozen places. Marichal won more games in the 1960s than anyone else. Three times he finished with at least 25 victories in a season.

WILL CLARK　　　　　　　First Baseman

• BORN: 3/13/1964　• PLAYED FOR TEAM: 1986 TO 1993

Will Clark was the heart and soul of the Giants for eight seasons in the 1980s and 1990s. His love of baseball inspired his teammates, and his lively bat won countless games for the team.

BARRY BONDS   Outfielder

- BORN: 7/24/1964
- PLAYED FOR TEAM: 1993 TO 2007

In 1992, Barry Bonds came "home" to the Giants. His father Bobby and godfather, Willie Mays, had starred for the team more than 20 years earlier. Bonds broke the single-season and career records for home runs and walks while playing for the Giants. He was voted NL MVP each year from 2001 to 2004.

BRIAN WILSON   Pitcher

- BORN: 3/16/1982
- FIRST YEAR WITH TEAM: 2006

Baseball fans knew Brian Wilson for his long, black beard. Opponents knew him for his great fastball and **slider**. In 2010, Wilson led the NL with 48 **saves**. Giants fans often brought signs to games that read, *Fear the Beard*.

TIM LINCECUM   Pitcher

- BORN: 6/15/1984   • FIRST YEAR WITH TEAM: 2007

Tim Lincecum got the nickname "The Freak" because of his skinny body and unusual pitching style. He amazed fans with the speed and control of his pitches. Lincecum led the NL in strikeouts each year from 2008 to 2010. He won the Cy Young Award in 2008 and 2009.

LEFT: Willie McCovey
ABOVE: Barry Bonds

CALLING THE SHOTS

The Giants are known for hiring smart and tricky managers who can give their team an extra edge. Over the years, many good leaders have worked in the Giants' dugout. Bill Terry, Alvin Dark, Charlie Fox, Roger Craig, Dusty Baker, and Felipe Alou all guided the team to first-place finishes. Baker set a record by winning 103 games in his first year. In 2010, Bruce Bochy led the Giants to their first World Series championship since moving to San Francisco in 1958.

One of the Giants' most beloved managers was Leo Durocher. "Leo the Lip" never stopped talking. He would do or say almost anything to upset opposing players, or to build up the confidence of his own players. In 1951, Willie Mays was a 20-year-old rookie. When he struggled at the plate, he began to wonder whether he belonged in the big leagues. Durocher told Mays that he would play no matter what. Mays went on to become **Rookie of the Year**, and the Giants won the pennant. Durocher led the Giants to another pennant in 1954.

Of all the managers to wear the Giants' uniform, the greatest by far was John McGraw. During his playing days, McGraw was

John McGraw hits grounders during a practice in the early 1920s.

known as the most clever man in baseball. After joining the Giants in 1902, he was hailed as the smartest manager. McGraw led the Giants for three decades. His teams finished first or second 21 times, and they won three World Series. He is one of only four managers in history to win more than 2,500 games.

Today's fans may find it strange, but a century ago people came to the ballpark to watch McGraw manage. He always had a new trick up his sleeve. He loved to surprise people by taking chances. He was famous for getting umpires to make calls in his favor. McGraw also liked to give unwanted players a chance. Sometimes it worked out, and sometimes it didn't. With McGraw, Giants fans truly came to expect the unexpected.

ONE GREAT DAY

There is no clock ticking during a baseball game. A team cannot win or lose until the final inning is played—and the final out is made. In 1951, the Giants and Brooklyn Dodgers battled all summer for the pennant. After 154 games, the two teams were tied with 96 wins each. The rules at the time said that the teams had to have a playoff—the first to win two games would be the NL champion.

The Giants won the first game 3–1 in Brooklyn's ballpark. The Dodgers won the next game 10–0. The third and final game was played on the Giants' home field, the Polo Grounds. The score was tied after seven innings. In the top of the eighth inning, the Dodgers scored three times.

The Dodgers held a 4–1 lead in the bottom of the ninth. Brooklyn's pitcher, Don Newcombe, was exhausted. He gave up singles to Alvin Dark and Don Mueller. Monte Irvin popped out,

LEFT: This souvenir celebrates the team's magical 1951 season. RIGHT: Bobby Thomson waves to the crowd moments after his famous home run.

but Whitey Lockman drilled a double that brought Dark home. The score was now 4–2.

The Dodgers brought in Ralph Branca to face Bobby Thomson. Branca threw a fastball over the plate, and Thomson watched it go by for strike one. Branca threw his next pitch high and inside. He did not expect Thomson to swing at it—he was hoping to get him out with his next pitch, a curveball.

But Thomson swung and hit a line drive to left field. Everyone waited for the ball to bounce off the wall, but instead it cleared the fence. With one swing of the bat, Thomson had given the Giants a 5–4 victory!

"The Giants win the pennant! The Giants win the pennant!" cried radio announcer Russ Hodges. Thomson circled the bases and was hugged by his teammates when he reached home plate. His "shot heard 'round the world" is still one of the most famous home runs in baseball history.

LEGEND HAS IT

WHICH GIANT WAS NICKNAMED AFTER A CARTOON CHARACTER?

LEGEND HAS IT that Pablo Sandoval was. When Sandoval first joined the Giants, he did not look like other rookies. Instead of being long and lean, he was squat and round. Even so, he was very athletic, and he pounded enemy pitching. Teammate Barry Zito took one look at Sandoval and decided he should be called "Kung Fu Panda." San Francisco fans loved it. Sandoval got to like it, too. It was certainly better than another nickname he had heard—the "Round Mound of Pound."

ABOVE: Pablo Sandoval
RIGHT: Arlie Latham

WHO WAS BASEBALL'S FIRST FULL-TIME COACH?

LEGEND HAS IT that Arlie Latham was. In the early days of baseball, older players often helped the manager with coaching duties. In 1907, John McGraw hired Latham to help him run the Giants. Latham had been a star in the 1890s and was known for his *practical jokes*. He kept the Giants "loose" under the strict McGraw.

WHO HAD BASEBALL'S MOST FAMOUS BEARD?

LEGEND HAS IT that Brian Wilson did. As the Giants closed in on their 2010 championship, Wilson started to let his beard grow. He also dyed it dark black. Soon fans were showing up at the ballpark with long black beards. Wilson also had a Mohawk-style hair cut. Not as many fans copied that. Wilson's beard became so famous that it had its own commercials. One took fans "inside Brian Wilson's beard," where they saw lumberjacks, Irish dancers, and a ninja.

Can one player make the difference between a losing season and a championship season? The Giants found out the answer in 2010. That year, San Francisco had two excellent pitchers, Tim Lincecum and Matt Cain. They also had Brian Wilson in the bullpen. But to win games, a team needs hitting. To win a championship, a team sometimes needs even more than that.

The 2010 Giants may not have had any superstars in the batting order, but their players had two important things—experience and pride. They got hits when they needed them, and they did all the little things it takes to win in the big leagues. Also, the Giants ran the bases well and didn't make mistakes when they were in the field.

The player who made the greatest difference for the Giants was not a veteran. He was a 23-year-old rookie named Buster Posey. He joined the team at the end of May and became the everyday catcher in June. At the beginning of July, the Giants started a long **road trip**. Posey hit six homers and drove in 15 runs during that stretch. When the team returned to San Francisco, the players and coaches began to

Buster Posey and Brian Wilson signed this magazine cover, which shows them moments after the final out of the 2010 World Series.

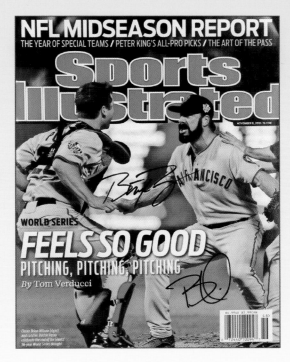

think they could make it to the World Series—even though they were in fourth place in the **NL West**!

Posey kept hitting, and the Giants kept winning. In September, San Francisco moved into first place and finished as NL West champs. Posey led the team with a .305 batting average. He hit 18 homers and drove in 67 runs in just over 100 games. Equally impressive was how well Posey handled San Francisco's pitchers. A young catcher does not always understand what pitches to call during a game, or how to get the most out of the men on the mound. Posey played his position like a veteran.

Posey caught every inning of every game in the playoffs and World Series. He continued to get big hits and make big plays on the way to the championship. After the World Series, Posey was named Rookie of the Year.

B aseball fans can have short memories. Once a player leaves the team, they often forget about all the times he made them stand up and cheer. This is not true of the Giants and their fans. In fact, they build statues in honor of their best players. Even young fans who never saw Willie McCovey, Willie Mays, Orlando Cepeda, or Juan Marichal recognize them the moment they enter the Giants' ballpark. It's easy because they've been told countless stories by their parents and grandparents.

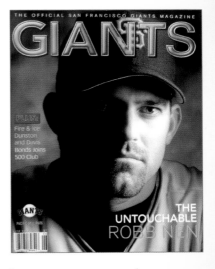

In recent years, people all over the country have gotten to know Giants fans. They watched them cheer for Barry Bonds as he broke home run records. They saw San Francisco fans pull black beards out of their pockets when Brian Wilson came in to pitch. They followed the kayakers in McCovey Cove as they paddled after home run balls. They learned it's a lot of fun to go to a Giants game!

LEFT: San Francisco fans say farewell to Barry Bonds in his final game.
ABOVE: A Giants game program shows Robb Nen, who led the NL in saves in 2001.

TIMELINE

Frankie Frisch was the leader of the 1924 Giants.

1883
The Giants join the National League.

1924
The Giants become the first NL team to win four pennants in a row.

1888
Tim Keefe wins 19 games in a row and leads the Giants to the pennant.

1903
John McGraw is hired to manage the team.

1930
Bill Terry is the last National Leaguer to bat .400 in a season.

Tim Keefe

John McGraw

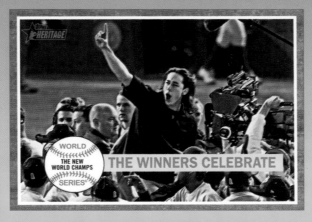

This trading card shows Tim Lincecum telling the world, "We're number one!"

1963
The Alou brothers—Felipe, Matty, and Jesus—play together in the Giants' outfield.

1998
Barry Bonds becomes the first player to hit 400 homers and steal 400 bases.

2010
The Giants win the World Series.

1961
Willie Mays hits four home runs in a game.

1974
Bobby Bonds wins his third Gold Glove in four seasons.

2007
Barry Bonds sets the all-time home run record.

Bobby Bonds

Barry Bonds

FUN FACTS

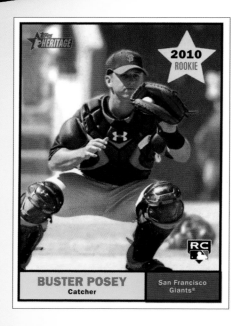

JUST A KID

In 2010, Buster Posey became the first rookie catcher to start for a World Series champion since 1966.

OUT OF THIS WORLD

Gaylord Perry was a good pitcher for the Giants, but a poor hitter. His manager predicted that a man would land on the moon before Perry launched a home run. In 1969, Perry hit his first homer—a few hours after astronaut Neil Armstrong stepped on the moon.

RISING SUN

In 1964 and 1965, Masanori Murakami was a member of the Giants' pitching staff. He was the first Japanese player in the major leagues.

ABOVE: This 2010 trading card shows Buster Posey as a rookie.
RIGHT: "Take Me Out to the Ballgame" is sung by fans in almost every baseball stadium.

THE WRITE STUFF

When Leo Durocher managed the Giants, he was married to a famous actress named Laraine Day. She wrote a book about being a manager's wife called *Day with the Giants*.

STARTING FIVE

When the Baseball **Hall of Fame** announced its first five members in 1936, Christy Mathewson was one of two pitchers in the group. The other was Walter Johnson.

SWEET MUSIC

Songwriter Jack Norworth got the idea for "Take Me Out to the Ballgame" while riding past the Giants' stadium on a subway. He did not actually go to his first baseball game until many years later.

THE SENSATIONAL BASE BALL SONG

TAKE ME OUT TO THE BALL GAME

WORDS BY JACK NORWORTH

MUSIC BY ALBERT VON TILZER

THE YORK MUSIC CO.
ALBERT VON TILZER, Mgr.
40 WEST 28TH ST. N.Y.

FAST COMPANY

In 2010, Tim Lincecum became the second Giant to lead the NL in strikeouts three years in a row. Christy Mathewson was the first. He did it from 1903 to 1905.

"Do I look crazy enough to jump into a cove? Come on, you've got to be kidding me! Why would I do a thing like that?"
▶ **WILLIE McCOVEY**, ON WHETHER HE WOULD CHASE A HOME RUN BALL HIT INTO McCOVEY COVE

"They throw the ball, I hit it. They hit the ball, I catch it."
▶ **WILLIE MAYS**, ON KEEPING THINGS SIMPLE

"You can learn little from victory. You can learn everything from defeat."
▶ **CHRISTY MATHEWSON**, ON THE WAY HE TAUGHT HIMSELF TO BE A BETTER PITCHER

ABOVE: Willie McCovey   **RIGHT**: Jeff Kent

"Winning is the only thing that makes me happy."

▶ *JEFF KENT, ON WHAT DROVE HIM DURING HIS PLAYING DAYS*

"I looked at Will every day and knew he was going to do something outstanding."

▶ *KEVIN MITCHELL, ON HIS TEAMMATE WILL "THE THRILL" CLARK*

"Get in front of those balls, you won't get hurt. That's what you've got a chest for."

▶ *JOHN McGRAW, ON THE CORRECT WAY TO FIELD A GROUND BALL*

"You've got to be a little crazy."

▶ *BRIAN WILSON, ON WHAT IT TAKES TO CLOSE OUT GAMES IN THE BIG LEAGUES.*

GREAT DEBATES

People who root for the Giants love to compare their favorite moments, teams, and players. Some debates have been going on for years! How would you settle these classic baseball arguments?

BARRY BONDS WAS THE GIANTS' BEST ALL-AROUND PLAYER ...

... because he hit for a high average and power, stole bases, and played good defense. Bonds set records for the most home runs in a season and in a career. He won two batting championships with the Giants and five Gold Gloves. Bonds also had a 40-homer, 40-steal season in 1996 and won the MVP award each year from 2001 to 2004. And what a batting eye—he led the NL in walks 11 times in the 15 seasons he played in San Francisco.

SAY HEY! WILLIE MAYS COULD RUN CIRCLES AROUND BONDS ...

... because he was a faster, stronger, and better player. Some say Mays (**LEFT**) was the best to ever play the game. Bonds was a great hitter, but so was Mays. Except when Mays hit the ball— Pow!—it sounded like a rifle shot. Both players were terrific fielders, but Mays played center field, the most important position in the outfield. And Mays won 11 Gold Gloves.

THE GIANTS' 2010 PITCHING STAFF WAS THE BEST IN TEAM HISTORY ...

... because they had four top starters, plus the league's best **closer**. Tim Lincecum, Matt Cain, Jonathan Sanchez, and Madison Bumgarner threw hard and also had good **breaking pitches**. As a group, they struck out more than a batter an inning. Brian Wilson saved 48 games in 2010. During the playoffs and World Series, they were even better!

MAYBE THE BEST IN SAN FRANCISCO HISTORY, BUT NOT IN GIANTS HISTORY ...

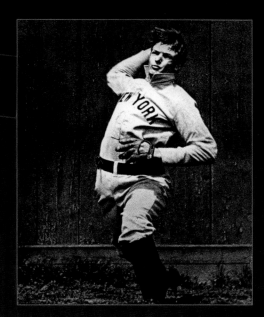

... because Christy Mathewson (RIGHT) and Carl Hubbell pitched for the Giants when they played in New York. Many believe Mathewson was the best right-hander in history. Some think Hubbell was the best left-hander. Both had great teammates. In 1904, Mathewson and Joe McGinnity won more than 30 games each, and Luther Taylor had another 21 victories. In 1933, Hubbell joined forces with Hal Schumacher and Freddie Fitzsimmons to win 58 games and lead New York to the championship.

The great Giants teams and players have left their marks on the record books. These are the "best of the best" …

John Montefusco

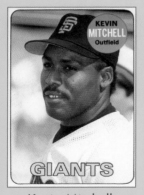

Kevin Mitchell

GIANTS AWARD WINNERS

WINNER	AWARD	YEAR
Carl Hubbell	Most Valuable Player	1933
Carl Hubbell	Most Valuable Player	1936
Willie Mays	Rookie of the Year	1951
Dusty Rhodes	World Series MVP	1954
Willie Mays	Most Valuable Player	1954
Orlando Cepeda	Rookie of the Year	1958
Willie McCovey	Rookie of the Year	1959
Willie Mays	All-Star Game MVP	1963
Juan Marichal	All-Star Game MVP	1965
Willie Mays	Most Valuable Player	1965
Mike McCormick	Cy Young Award	1967
Willie Mays	All-Star Game MVP	1968
Willie McCovey	All-Star Game MVP	1969
Willie McCovey	Most Valuable Player	1969
Bobby Bonds	All-Star Game MVP	1973
Gary Matthews	Rookie of the Year	1973
John Montefusco	Rookie of the Year	1975
Kevin Mitchell	Most Valuable Player	1989
Dusty Baker	Manager of the Year	1993
Barry Bonds	Most Valuable Player	1993
Dusty Baker	Manager of the Year	1997
Dusty Baker	Manager of the Year	2000
Jeff Kent	Most Valuable Player	2000
Barry Bonds	Most Valuable Player	2001
Barry Bonds	Most Valuable Player	2002
Barry Bonds	Most Valuable Player	2003
Barry Bonds	Most Valuable Player	2004
Tim Lincecum	Cy Young Award	2008
Tim Lincecum	Cy Young Award	2009
Buster Posey	Rookie of the Year	2010
Edgar Renteria	World Series MVP	2010

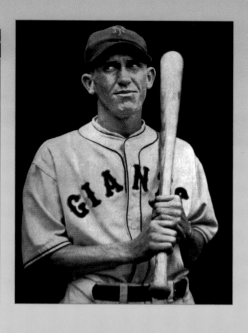

ACHIEVEMENT	YEAR
NL Pennant Winners	1888
World Series Champions	1888
NL Pennant Winners	1889
World Series Champions	1889
NL Pennant Winners	1904
NL Pennant Winners	1905
World Series Champions	1905
NL Pennant Winners	1911
NL Pennant Winners	1912
NL Pennant Winners	1913
NL Pennant Winners	1917
NL Pennant Winners	1921
World Series Champions	1921
NL Pennant Winners	1922
World Series Champions	1922
NL Pennant Winners	1923
NL Pennant Winners	1924
NL Pennant Winners	1933
World Series Champions	1933
NL Pennant Winners	1936
NL Pennant Winners	1937
NL Pennant Winners	1951
NL Pennant Winners	1954
World Series Champions	1954
NL Pennant Winners	1962
NL West Champions	1971
NL West Champions	1987
NL West Champions	1989
NL Pennant Winners	1989
NL West Champions	1997
NL West Champions	2000
NL Pennant Winners	2002
NL West Champions	2003
NL West Champions	2010
NL Pennant Winners	2010
World Series Champions	2010

BRUCE BOCHY
MANAGER • SAN FRANCISCO

TOP: Jo-Jo Moore was the center fielder on the pennant-winning teams of the 1930s.　　**RIGHT**: Bruce Bochy led the Giants to their first championship since 1954.

43

PINPOINTS

The history of a baseball team is made up of many smaller stories. These stories take place all over the map—not just in the city a team calls "home." Match the pushpins on these maps to the **TEAM FACTS**, and you will begin to see the story of the Giants unfold!

TEAM FACTS

1 San Francisco, California—*The Giants have played here since 1958.*
2 Sioux City, Iowa—*Dave Bancroft was born here.*
3 Cleveland, Ohio—*The Giants won the 1954 World Series here.*
4 Factoryville, Pennsylvania—*Christy Mathewson was born here.*
5 New York, New York—*The Giants played here from 1883 to 1957.*
6 Carthage, Missouri—*Carl Hubbell was born here.*
7 Williamston, North Carolina—*Gaylord Perry was born here.*
8 Arlington, Texas—*The Giants won the 2010 World Series here.*
9 Westfield, Alabama—*Willie Mays was born here.*
10 West Palm Beach, Florida—*Robby Thompson was born here.*
11 Bajos de Haina, San Cristobal, Dominican Republic—*Felipe Alou was born here.*
12 Glasgow, Scotland—*Bobby Thomson was born here.*

Felipe Alou

45

GLOSSARY

BREAKING PITCHES—Pitches that move as they near home plate, such as a curveball.

BULLPEN—The area where a team's relief pitchers warm up. This word also describes the group of relief pitchers in this area.

CLOSER—A pitcher who finishes (or "closes") games for his team.

CONTENDERS—People who compete for a championship.

CY YOUNG AWARD— The award given each year to each league's best pitcher.

DECADES—Periods of 10 years; also specific periods, such as the 1950s.

HALL OF FAME—The museum in Cooperstown, New York, where baseball's greatest players are honored.

MOST VALUABLE PLAYER (MVP)— The award given each year to each league's top player; an MVP is also selected for the World Series and the All-Star Game.

NATIONAL LEAGUE (NL)—The older of the two major leagues; the NL began play in 1876.

NATIONAL LEAGUE CHAMPIONSHIP SERIES (NLCS)—The playoff series that has decided the National League pennant since 1969.

NEGRO LEAGUES—Baseball leagues organized and run by African-Americans. Major League Baseball did not welcome black players until 1947.

NL WEST—A group of National League teams that play in the western part of the country.

PENNANTS—League championships. The term comes from the triangular flag awarded to each season's champion, beginning in the 1870s.

PLAYER-MANAGER—A player who also manages his team.

PLAYOFFS—The games played after the regular season to determine which teams will advance to the World Series.

POSTSEASON—The games played after the regular season, including the playoffs and World Series.

PRACTICAL JOKES—Jokes played on people not expecting them.

ROAD TRIP—A series of games played away from home.

ROOKIE—A player in his first season.

ROOKIE OF THE YEAR—The annual award given to each league's best first-year player.

SAVES—A statistic that counts the number of times a relief pitcher finishes off a close victory for his team.

SHUTOUT—A game in which one team does not score a run.

SLIDER—A fast pitch that curves and drops just as it reaches the batter.

STARTING ROTATION—The group of pitchers who take turns beginning games for their team. These pitchers are often called "starters."

VETERANS—Players who have great experience.

WORLD SERIES—The world championship series played between the American League and National League pennant winners.

EXTRA INNINGS

TEAM SPIRIT introduces a great way to stay up to date with your team! Visit our **EXTRA INNINGS** link and get connected to the latest and greatest updates. **EXTRA INNINGS** serves as a young reader's ticket to an exclusive web page—with more stories, fun facts, team records, and photos of the Giants. Content is updated during and after each season. The **EXTRA INNINGS** feature also enables readers to send comments and letters to the author! Log onto:

www.norwoodhousepress.com/library.aspx

and click on the tab: **TEAM SPIRIT** to access **EXTRA INNINGS**.

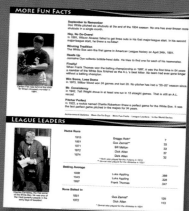

Read all the books in the series to learn more about professional sports. For a complete listing of the baseball, basketball, football, and hockey teams in the **TEAM SPIRIT** series, visit our website at:

www.norwoodhousepress.com/library.aspx

ON THE ROAD

SAN FRANCISCO GIANTS
24 Willie Mays Plaza
San Francisco, California 94107
(408) 297-1435
sanfrancisco.giants.mlb.com

**NATIONAL BASEBALL
HALL OF FAME AND MUSEUM**
25 Main Street
Cooperstown, New York 13326
(888) 425-5633
www.baseballhalloffame.org

ON THE BOOKSHELF

To learn more about the sport of baseball, look for these books at your library or bookstore:

- Augustyn, Adam (editor). *The Britannica Guide to Baseball*. New York, NY: Rosen Publishing, 2011.

- Dreier, David. *Baseball: How It Works*. North Mankato, MN: Capstone Press, 2010.

- Stewart, Mark. *Ultimate 10: Baseball*. New York, NY: Gareth Stevens Publishing, 2009.

INDEX

PAGE NUMBERS IN **BOLD** REFER TO ILLUSTRATIONS.

Alou, Felipe................9, 24, 35, **45**
Alou, Jesus................................35
Alou, Matty...............................35
Ames, Red...................................7
Armstrong, Neil...........................36
Baker, Dusty..........................24, 42
Bancroft, Dave..........................7, 45
Barnes, Jesse..............................7
Beck, Rod.................................10
Bochy, Bruce.........................24, **43**
Bonds, Barry.........9, **9**, 10, 13, 23,
    23, **32**, 33, 35, **35**, 40, 42
Bonds, Bobby...........23, 35, **35**, 42
Branca, Ralph............................27
Bresnahan, Roger..........................7
Bumgarner, Madison...........11, 19, 41
Cain, Matt..........11, **14**, 19, 30, 41
Cepeda, Orlando...............9, 33, 42
Clark, Will.....................9, 22, 39
Connor, Roger...........................6, 16
Craig, Roger.............................24
Dark, Alvin...................24, 26, 27
Day, Laraine.............................37
Doyle, Larry..............................7
Durocher, Leo.........................24, 37
Ewing, Buck.............................6, 16
Fitzsimmons, Freddie.....................41
Fox, Charlie.............................24
Frisch, Frankie...............7, **16**, **34**
Gore, George.............................16
Groh, Heinie.............................**16**
Hodges, Russ.............................27
Hubbell, Carl..................7, **15**, 17,
    21, 41, 42, 45
Huff, Aubrey.............................11
Irvin, Monte...........................7, 26
Jackson, Travis........................7, **16**
Johnson, Walter..........................37
Keefe, Tim..........6, 16, 20, 34, **34**
Kelly, George..........................7, **16**
Kent, Jeff...........9, 10, 39, **39**, 42
Latham, Arlie.........................29, **29**
Lincecum, Tim...........10, **10**, 11, 18,
    23, 30, **35**, 37, 41, 42
Lockman, Whitey..........................27
Marichal, Juan.............9, 22, 33, 42
Marquard, Rube...........................7

Mathewson, Christy..........7, 11, 16,
    20, 37, 38, 41, **41**, 45
Matthews, Gary...........................42
Mays, Willie.................7, **8**, 9, 11,
    17, 21, 23, 24, 33,
    35, 38, 40, **40**, 42, 45
McCormick, Mike..........................42
McCovey, Willie..............9, 22, **22**,
    33, 38, **38**, 42
McGinnity, Joe.........................7, 41
McGraw, John.............6, **6**, 7, 16,
    17, 24, 25, **25**, 29, 34, **34**, 39
Mitchell, Kevin.........9, 10, 39, 42, **42**
Montefusco, John.....................42, **42**
Moore, Jo-Jo.............................**43**
Mueller, Don.............................26
Murakami, Masanori.......................36
Mutrie, Jim...............................6
Nen, Robb.............................10, **33**
Newcombe, Don............................26
Norworth, Jack...........................37
Ott, Mel....................7, **7**, 17, 21
Perry, Gaylord...................9, 36, 45
Posey, Buster..................11, 18, 30,
    31, **31**, 36, **36**, 42
Renteria, Edgar..............19, **19**, 42
Rhodes, Dusty...............17, **17**, 42
Ross, Cody...........................18, **18**
Sanchez, Freddy..........................11
Sanchez, Jonathan.....................11, 41
Sandoval, Pablo.............11, 28, **28**
Schumacher, Hal..............7, 17, 41
Taylor, Luther...........................41
Terry, Bill.....................7, 17,
    21, **21**, 24, 34
Thompson, Hank............................7
Thompson, Robby........................9, 45
Thomson, Bobby............27, **27**, 45
Tiernan, Mike............................16
Ward, John.............................6, 16
Welch, Mickey..........................6, 16
Williams, Matt............................9
Wilson, Brian................11, **11**, 19, 23,
    29, 30, **31**, 33, 39, 41
Wiltse, George............................7
Youngs, Ross..............................7
Zito, Barry..............................28

ABOUT THE AUTHOR

MARK STEWART has written more than 50 books on baseball and over 150 sports books for kids. He grew up in New York City during the 1960s rooting for the Yankees and Mets, and was lucky enough to meet players from both teams. Mark comes from a family of writers. His grandfather was Sunday Editor of *The New York Times,* and his mother was Articles Editor of *Ladies' Home Journal* and *McCall's.* Mark has profiled hundreds of athletes over the past 25 years. He has also written several books about his native New York and New Jersey, his home today. Mark is a graduate of Duke University, with a degree in history. He lives and works in a home overlooking Sandy Hook, New Jersey. You can contact Mark through the Norwood House Press website.